Mind Matters

Navigating the Top 10 Mental Health Needs"

Dr. Jose De La Rosa

Edited and proofread by Dr. Jose De La Rosa.

Book cover designed by Dr. Jose De La Rosa

Printed in the United States of America.

Table of Contents

Mind Matters

Navigating the Top 10 Mental Health Needs"

Introduction

Navigating the Inner Landscape

In a world that often prioritizes physical health above all else, it's easy to overlook an equally vital aspect of our well-being: our mental health. Our minds are intricate, delicate, and powerful instruments, guiding us through the labyrinth of life's challenges and triumphs. Yet, too often, they go unnoticed until they start to falter, and we find ourselves grappling with overwhelming emotions, anxiety, or depression.

This is where "Mind Matters" steps in—a guiding light amidst the shadows that sometimes cloud our mental landscape. Welcome to a journey that delves deep into the realms of our consciousness, illuminating the intricacies of the human mind and offering you a roadmap to navigate the top ten mental health needs that impact us all.

The Weight of Silence

Mental health has long been shrouded in silence, stigma, and misconceptions. For too many, it remains an uncharted territory, leaving countless individuals to silently bear the weight of their emotional burdens. The repercussions of this silence are far-reaching, affecting not only individuals but entire communities, workplaces, and societies.

However, the tide is turning. Conversations about mental health are slowly breaking free from the chains of stigma, and the acknowledgment of our psychological well-being as an essential part of our overall health is gaining momentum. People from all walks of life are speaking up, sharing their stories, and seeking help. "Mind Matters" is a testament to this changing landscape, offering a comprehensive guide that aims to empower, educate, and inspire.

The Power of Understanding

Understanding mental health needs is a critical step toward fostering a society that values the well-being of every individual. When we grasp the complexities of our minds and the needs they harbor, we become better equipped to support ourselves and those around us. We cease to see mental health as a separate realm, detached from our daily lives, and instead embrace it as an integral part of our existence.

"Mind Matters" embarks on this journey of understanding, unraveling the intricate tapestry of our mental needs. From managing anxiety to recovering from trauma, from cultivating resilience to nurturing self-esteem, this book will be your guide through the labyrinth of mental health.

The Blueprint of "Mind Matters

Each chapter of "Mind Matters" is dedicated to exploring a specific mental health need, drawing on a combination of research, expert insights, and the lived experiences of individuals who have navigated these challenges. You'll find practical strategies, coping mechanisms, and guidance on how to address and overcome these needs. Moreover, this book serves as a beacon of hope, reminding you that you are not alone on this journey.

In the pages that follow, we will dive deep into the following ten mental health needs:

1. **Anxiety Management:** Understanding and effectively managing anxiety to regain control over your life.
2. **Depression Treatment:** Exploring treatments and strategies to combat depression and embrace a life of vitality.
3. **Trauma Recovery:** Navigating the path to recovery and healing from the wounds of trauma.
4. **Stress Coping Strategies:** Equipping yourself with tools to manage stress and build resilience.
5. **Emotional Regulation Skills:** Mastering the art of understanding and controlling your emotions.
6. **Self-esteem Building:** Cultivating a strong sense of self-worth and self-compassion.
7. **Addiction Recovery:** Breaking free from the grip of addiction and finding a path to sobriety.
8. **Social Connection and Community:** Building meaningful connections and forging a supportive community.
9. **Mindfulness and Self-Awareness:** Harnessing the power of mindfulness to enhance self-awareness and inner peace.
10. **Resilience and Coping Skills:** Strengthening your resilience and honing your coping skills to face life's challenges head-on.

Your Mental Health Journey

This book is not just about knowledge; it's about transformation. It's about taking the first step on your mental health journey or enhancing the path you're already on. It's about finding the strength to speak your truth, seek help when needed, and create a world where mental health is not just a priority but a fundamental right.

As we embark on this exploration together, remember that you are not alone in your struggles or your victories. Countless individuals have walked this path before you, and they have left a trail of wisdom, resilience, and hope. "Mind Matters" is your guide to their collective wisdom, offering a roadmap to brighter days and a healthier mind.

So, let us journey together through the pages of this book, where the intricacies of your mind will be revealed, your spirit will be fortified, and your heart will be uplifted. Together, we will navigate the top ten mental health needs, and in doing so, we will not only discover the power of our minds but also the boundless strength within ourselves.

Welcome to "Mind Matters: Navigating the Top 10 Mental Health Needs." Let our journey begin.

Defining the Purpose of "Mind Matters Navigating the Top 10 Mental Health Needs"

In a world where the demands of daily life often overshadow the importance of mental well-being, "Mind Matters: Navigating the Top 10 Mental Health Needs" emerges as a beacon of understanding, guidance, and hope. This book is not merely a collection of words on paper; it is a compass, pointing readers toward the profound and complex landscape of their own minds. At its core, the purpose of this book is to shed light on the intricacies of mental health, offering insight, support, and practical tools to navigate the top ten mental health needs that touch the lives of countless individuals around the world.

The Crisis of Mental Health

Mental health, often relegated to the shadows of public discourse, has been undergoing a quiet crisis for far too long. The statistics paint a stark picture: depression, anxiety disorders, and other mental health challenges are on the rise globally, affecting people of all ages, backgrounds, and walks of life. According to the World Health Organization, depression is now the leading cause of disability worldwide, and anxiety disorders are not far behind. Yet, despite the prevalence of these issues, many still grapple with the weight of silence and stigma that surrounds mental health.

The purpose of "Mind Matters" is to shatter this silence. It aims to dismantle the stigma that has cast a long shadow over individuals living with mental health challenges and, in doing so, to initiate a candid and compassionate conversation. This book strives to bring mental health to the forefront, acknowledging it as a fundamental component of our overall well-being. By defining and addressing the top ten mental health needs, we seek to provide a roadmap to those who have felt lost in the labyrinth of their own minds.

Understanding the Purpose: A Deeper Dive

To truly grasp the purpose of "Mind Matters," we must dissect it into its essential components:

1. Education and Awareness: One of the primary objectives of this book is to educate. It serves as a compendium of knowledge, exploring the top ten mental health needs in-depth. Through comprehensive research, expert insights, and real-life stories, we aim to provide readers with a foundational understanding of these needs. By shedding light on the intricacies of mental health, we empower individuals to recognize, acknowledge, and address their own challenges or those of their loved ones.

2. Breaking the Stigma: The purpose of "Mind Matters" extends beyond knowledge to advocacy. We are committed to dismantling the stigma surrounding mental health issues. Stigma perpetuates silence, shame, and suffering. It is a barrier that prevents individuals from seeking help, opening up about their struggles, or accessing the support they need. By openly discussing and normalizing mental health conversations, we aim to erode the walls of stigma brick by brick, creating a more compassionate and inclusive society.

3. Practical Guidance: Knowledge alone is not enough. The purpose of this book is to provide practical guidance and actionable strategies. We recognize that understanding mental health needs is only the first step. To effect meaningful change, individuals require tools, coping mechanisms, and resources to navigate the challenges they face. Each chapter within "Mind Matters" is dedicated to exploring a specific mental health need, offering insights, advice, and evidence-based practices to empower readers in their journey toward better mental well-being.

4. Empowerment and Support: "Mind Matters" seeks to empower individuals to take control of their mental health journey. It encourages readers to become active participants in their own well-being, promoting self-advocacy and self-compassion. The purpose is to offer support not only through information but also by sharing the stories of resilience and recovery. These stories serve as a reminder that, no matter how daunting the challenges may seem, there is hope, and there is a path forward.

5. Community and Unity: Mental health affects us all, transcending geographical borders, cultural divides, and social hierarchies. The purpose of "Mind Matters" is to foster a sense of unity and community. It invites individuals from diverse backgrounds to come together in the shared recognition of our common humanity. By weaving the threads of our stories into a tapestry of understanding, we hope to create a supportive community where individuals can find solace, empathy, and the knowledge that they are not alone.

Conclusion: The Unveiling of Purpose

In its essence, "Mind Matters: Navigating the Top 10 Mental Health Needs" is a book that aims to serve humanity. It seeks to uplift, educate, and unite. It strives to be a trusted companion on the winding path of mental well-being. Its purpose is not only to inform but to transform lives, one reader at a time. We embark on this journey with the firm belief that by understanding and addressing our mental health needs, we can reclaim our inner strength, foster resilience, and build a world where mental health truly matters.

Dedication

To the Brave Souls Who Navigate the Storm

To the resilient hearts and enduring spirits,

This book is dedicated to you to each brave soul who awakens each day with the weight of the world resting upon your shoulders yet finds the strength to carry on. You, the unsung heroes of our world, who face the invisible battles of the mind with unwavering courage and determination, are the driving force behind "Mind Matters: Navigating the Top 10 Mental Health Needs."

In the vast tapestry of humanity, there exists a unique thread the thread of suffering, resilience, and hope—that binds us all together. It is your experiences, your stories, your struggles, and your triumphs that have woven this tapestry into a masterpiece of unwavering strength. It is your resilience in the face of adversity that inspires us to embark on this journey, to dive deep into the depths of your pain, and to rise together toward the shores of healing and well-being.

The Unseen Battles

Your battles are unlike any other, for they unfold within the labyrinthine corridors of your mind. The world may not always see the wars you wage, the scars you bear, or the tears you shed in the silent hours of the night. It may not hear the symphony of thoughts that orchestrate the symphony of your emotions, sometimes in harmonious melody, at other times in dissonant cacophony. Your pain may be invisible to the world, but it is achingly real to you.

We dedicate "Mind Matters" to you because we acknowledge the enormity of your struggle. We recognize the courage it takes to face each day, even when the darkness threatens to engulf you. We understand that your journey is not linear, and healing is not always swift. You are not alone in your suffering, and we are here to stand with you, to listen to you, and to offer our unwavering support.

A Collective Voice

In dedicating this book to you, we hope to amplify your voices the voices that have been silenced for far too long. We aim to transform the shadows that shroud mental health into a spotlight of understanding and compassion. Through your stories, your resilience, and your journey toward healing, we hope to convey a powerful message: you are not defined by your challenges, but by your strength in confronting them.

You, who wrestle with anxiety, carrying the weight of your worries on your shoulders, are not alone.

You, who battle the suffocating embrace of depression, seeking the light in the midst of darkness, are not alone.

You, who bear the scars of trauma, yet refuse to let it define your future, are not alone.

You, who grapple with the relentless grip of stress, finding ways to build resilience with each passing day, are not alone.

You, who navigate the turbulent seas of emotion, seeking balance and control, are not alone.

You, who are on a journey of self-discovery, piecing together the fragments of self-esteem, are not alone.

You, who fight the relentless pull of addiction, are not alone.

You, who yearn for meaningful connections and community, are not alone.

You, who embrace mindfulness and self-awareness as tools of empowerment, are not alone.

You, who embody the essence of resilience and the art of coping, are not alone.

A Collective Journey

Together, we embark on a collective journey—a journey toward understanding, healing, and well-being. "Mind Matters" is more than a book; it is a bridge that connects your experiences to the world's understanding. It is a testament to your courage and a tribute to your indomitable spirit.

May the pages of this book serve as a sanctuary—a place where you can find solace, guidance, and the knowledge that you are seen and heard. May the stories within these pages inspire you, and the practical strategies empower you to navigate the intricate labyrinth of your mind with grace and resilience.

As we dedicate "Mind Matters: Navigating the Top 10 Mental Health Needs" to you, our promise is simple: you are not alone in your journey. You are cherished, respected, and celebrated. Your struggles do not define you, but your resilience and strength do. Together, we will navigate the storm, and together, we will emerge into the light.

With boundless admiration and unwavering support,

Dr. Jose De La Rosa

Chapter 1

The Weight of Anxiety

In the quiet of the night, when the world is asleep, your mind races with thoughts that seem beyond your control. Your heart pounds, and a heavy feeling settles in your chest. Anxiety has come to visit again.

Anxiety the relentless companion that affects millions around the world, irrespective of age, gender, or background. It's a feeling that we've all experienced at some point in our lives a natural response to life's uncertainties and challenges. Yet, for many, anxiety transcends the occasional worry; it becomes a constant presence, a shadow that refuses to dissipate.

Understanding Anxiety

Anxiety is a complex and multifaceted emotion, one that can manifest in various forms and intensities. At its core, it's a response to perceived threats or dangers, triggering a surge of adrenaline, known as the "fight or flight" response, in our bodies. In moderation, anxiety can be a helpful and protective mechanism, alerting us to potential dangers and keeping us vigilant.

However, when anxiety spirals out of control, it becomes a burden rather than a benefit. This is the point where it infiltrates our daily lives, affecting our thoughts, emotions, and behaviors. It can manifest as generalized anxiety disorder (GAD), social anxiety disorder, specific phobias, panic disorder, or other forms, each with its unique set of challenges.

The Weight of Excessive Worry

Imagine waking up every morning with a sense of impending doom, your mind racing with what-ifs and worst-case scenarios. Imagine the unease that creeps in when you're among a crowd, making you question your every move and word. Imagine the physical symptoms racing heart, trembling hands, shortness of breath that accompany anxiety, making even the simplest tasks feel insurmountable.

This is the reality for those living with chronic anxiety. It's not merely a fleeting feeling of nervousness before a presentation or a job interview; it's an all-encompassing, pervasive presence that can erode one's quality of life. It's the relentless worry that refuses to be appeased, the unease that festers in the pit of the stomach.

The Faces of Anxiety

Anxiety wears many faces, and its manifestations vary from person to person. For some, it's the fear of public speaking that paralyzes them in professional settings. For others, it's the dread of social interactions that leads to isolation. It can also manifest as specific phobias, such as fear of flying, heights, or spiders, causing individuals to avoid situations that trigger their anxiety.

In some cases, anxiety can escalate into panic attacks—intense and sudden surges of fear and discomfort. These attacks can be so overwhelming that individuals may feel like they are losing control or experiencing a heart attack. The fear of having another panic attack can become a vicious cycle, further fueling anxiety.

The Cycle of Catastrophic Thinking

One of the defining features of anxiety is catastrophic thinking the tendency to imagine the worst possible outcomes in any given situation. It's as if your mind becomes a storyteller, weaving tales of doom and disaster. Every minor setback is perceived as a catastrophe, every challenge an insurmountable obstacle.

Catastrophic thinking feeds the anxiety cycle. It perpetuates a state of hyper-vigilance, where you are always on high alert, anticipating danger around every corner. This heightened state of arousal not only takes a toll on your mental well-being but also has physical consequences, such as increased heart rate, muscle tension, and disrupted sleep.

The Toll on Mental and Physical Health

Chronic anxiety, if left unaddressed, can wreak havoc on both mental and physical health. It's not a matter of mere discomfort; it's a significant contributor to mental health disorders, including depression. The constant strain of living with anxiety can lead to emotional exhaustion, isolation, and a reduced quality of life.

Furthermore, anxiety can take a toll on physical health. Prolonged stress and anxiety can weaken the immune system, increase the risk of cardiovascular problems, and lead to various other health issues. The mind-body connection is undeniable, and the toll that anxiety exacts on the body is a testament to this intricate relationship.

Seeking Relief and Support

The journey to managing anxiety begins with acknowledgment an acknowledgment that you are not alone in your struggle, that anxiety is a legitimate challenge, and that seeking help is not a sign of weakness but of courage.

If anxiety has become a constant companion in your life, it's essential to seek relief and support. Understanding that you have options and that help is available can be a beacon of hope. It's a recognition that you deserve to live a life not dictated by anxiety.

The Path to Anxiety Management

Anxiety management is a multifaceted journey that combines self-awareness, coping strategies, and, in many cases, professional support. It's about reclaiming control over your thoughts and emotions, reducing the impact of anxiety on your life, and fostering a sense of inner peace.

In the chapters that follow, we will explore anxiety in-depth, offering insights, practical strategies, and guidance for managing its various forms. We will delve into evidence-based approaches, mindfulness techniques, and coping mechanisms that empower you to navigate the intricate landscape of anxiety.

Remember, the weight of anxiety can be lightened, and the shadows it casts can be dispelled. You are not defined by your anxiety; you are defined by your strength in confronting it.

In the pages that follow, let us embark on a journey of understanding, healing, and resilience. Together, we will explore the depths of anxiety and emerge into the light of anxiety management.

The journey begins here.

Chapter 2

Unmasking Mental Health: A Guide to Thriving

In a world that often celebrates resilience in silence, it's time to break free from the mask of strength and embrace the beauty of vulnerability.

Imagine a society where mental health is as natural a topic of conversation as the weather, where individuals are free to express their emotions without fear of judgment, and where seeking help for mental well-being is not only accepted but encouraged. Such a society may seem like a utopian dream, but it is within our grasp. To turn this dream into a reality, we must begin by unmasking mental health.

The Mask of Strength

From an early age, we are taught to wear masks the masks of strength, composure, and invincibility.

We learn that showing vulnerability is a sign of weakness, and so we don our emotional armor, hiding our inner struggles from the world. These masks become our shield, protecting us from the perceived judgment of others and the vulnerability of exposing our true selves.

This societal conditioning extends to mental health. We are led to believe that acknowledging our mental struggles is a sign of inadequacy. As a result, many suffer in silence, trapped behind the mask of strength, even when they are crumbling within.

The Weight of Silence

The consequences of this silence are profound. When we conceal our mental health challenges, we isolate ourselves from the support and understanding we desperately need. We become prisoners of our own thoughts and emotions, unable to break free from the cycle of suffering.

The weight of silence presses down on individuals, families, and communities. It perpetuates the stigma surrounding mental health, reinforcing the idea that it is something to be hidden and ashamed of. The irony is that this silence only amplifies the pain, making it more challenging to seek help or find solace.

The Power of Vulnerability

Vulnerability is often misunderstood. It is not a weakness but a strength—a powerful force that connects us on a profound level. When we embrace vulnerability, we remove our masks, revealing our authentic selves to the world. In doing so, we invite genuine connections, empathy, and understanding.

Consider the impact of vulnerability in your own life. Think of a time when you opened up to a friend or loved one about your struggles, fears, or insecurities. What happened? More often than not, you were met with compassion and support. Vulnerability has the remarkable ability to elicit a human response, forging connections that transcend the superficial.

The Ripple Effect of Authenticity

Authenticity is the byproduct of vulnerability—an unfiltered expression of our thoughts, emotions, and experiences. When we embrace authenticity, we not only liberate ourselves from the shackles of pretense but also inspire those around us to do the same.

Picture a world where individuals feel free to discuss their mental health openly. The ripple effect of authenticity would be profound. It would break down the walls of stigma, encourage early intervention and support, and create a culture of understanding and empathy.

The Path to Thriving

Thriving is not merely the absence of mental health challenges; it is the presence of emotional well-being and resilience. To thrive, we must unmask mental health, creating a safe space for ourselves and others to acknowledge our struggles, seek help, and embrace authenticity.

Embracing Your Mental Health Journey

Your mental health journey is uniquely yours. It is a path of self-discovery, self-care, and self-compassion. Embracing this journey starts with the simple act of acknowledging your mental health, unmasking the emotions that lie beneath the surface.

1. **Self-Awareness:** Begin by becoming more self-aware. Pay attention to your thoughts, emotions, and behaviors. Take note of patterns and triggers. Self-awareness is the first step in recognizing when you need support.
2. **Self-Compassion:** Treat yourself with the same kindness and compassion that you would offer to a friend. Mental health challenges are not a sign of weakness or failure; they are a part of the human experience.
3. **Reach Out:** Seek support when needed. Whether it's through friends, family, or mental health professionals, reaching out is a courageous step toward healing and thriving.
4. **Share Your Story:** Consider sharing your mental health journey with someone you trust. You may be surprised by the empathy and support you receive in return.

Creating a Culture of Authenticity

To unmask mental health on a broader scale, we must collectively work toward creating a culture of authenticity. Here are some steps we can take:

1. **Normalize Conversations:** Encourage open conversations about mental health in your family, workplace, and community. Normalize discussions about emotions, stress, and well-being.
2. **Educate and Advocate:** Learn about mental health, the importance of seeking help, and the available resources. Advocate for mental health awareness and access to mental health care.
3. **Support Each Other:** Be a source of support for those around you. Listen without judgment, offer a compassionate ear, and encourage seeking professional help when needed.
4. **Lead by Example:** Embrace vulnerability and authenticity in your own life. By leading by example, you inspire others to do the same.

Conclusion: Unmasking Mental Health for a Thriving World

"Mind Matters: Navigating the Top 10 Mental Health Needs" is not just a book; it is a call to action. It is a call to unmask mental health, to embrace vulnerability, and to create a world where individuals can thrive.

As we delve deeper into the mental health needs discussed in this book, remember that your mental health journey is a testament to your strength. By unmasking mental health, you contribute to a culture of understanding, support, and authenticity.

The path to thriving begins with the courage to be yourself, vulnerabilities and all. Together, we can unmask mental health and pave the way for a world where every individual can thrive.

The journey of unmasking mental health starts now.

Chapter 3

Healing Minds: Strategies for Mental Well-Being

In the labyrinth of the mind, there are paths to healing and hope. Let us embark on a journey to discover these transformative strategies for mental well-being.

Life is an intricate tapestry of experiences, emotions, and challenges. At times, the threads of our tapestry become tangled, leading to inner turmoil and distress. This is where the art of healing minds comes into play a collection of strategies, tools, and practices that can help us navigate the complexities of our mental well-being.

The Power of Healing

Healing is a profound and transformative process—a journey of self-discovery, resilience, and growth. It is not about erasing the scars of our past or escaping the challenges of the present, but about finding strength and meaning in the midst of adversity. Healing is the restoration of our inner equilibrium, the mending of our emotional wounds, and the rekindling of hope.

In the realm of mental health, healing is not a destination but a continuous journey a path toward greater well-being, emotional stability, and inner peace. It's about learning to manage, cope with, and transcend the challenges that life presents. To embark on this journey, we must equip ourselves with strategies that empower us to heal our minds and nurture our mental health.

Understanding Mental Well-Being

Mental well-being is not the absence of challenges or negative emotions. It is the ability to navigate life's ups and downs with resilience, self-awareness, and a sense of balance. It's about cultivating a positive relationship with ourselves and our experiences, even when faced with adversity.

Mental well-being encompasses various aspects of our lives, including our emotions, thoughts, relationships, and overall satisfaction with life. It is not a one-size-fits-all concept but a deeply personal and evolving experience. What promotes well-being for one person may differ for another, making it essential to explore and discover the strategies that work best for you.

Holistic Well-Being: Mind, Body, and Spirit

To foster mental well-being, we must recognize the interconnectedness of our mind, body, and spirit. These facets of our being are not separate entities but interconnected aspects of our overall health. Strategies for mental well-being extend beyond the mind, encompassing physical health, self-care, and spiritual nourishment.

1. **Physical Well-Being:** Regular exercise, balanced nutrition, and adequate sleep are fundamental to mental well-being. Physical activity releases endorphins, which boost mood and reduce stress. Proper nutrition provides essential nutrients for brain function, and quality sleep is crucial for emotional regulation and cognitive function.
2. **Self-Care:** Self-care involves intentionally setting aside time for activities that promote relaxation and joy. It may include hobbies, mindfulness practices, creative expression, or spending time in nature. Self-care is not indulgent but essential for recharging and maintaining mental well-being.
3. **Spiritual Nourishment:** Spiritual well-being can encompass religious beliefs, but it also extends to a sense of purpose, connection to nature, or a broader perspective on life. Nurturing your spiritual dimension can provide a source of comfort and meaning during challenging times.

Strategies for Healing Minds

The strategies for healing minds are diverse, offering a range of tools to promote mental well-being and resilience. Here are some key strategies to explore:

1. **Mindfulness and Meditation:** Mindfulness practices, such as meditation, help cultivate self-awareness, reduce stress, and enhance emotional regulation. These practices encourage us to be present in the moment, observe our thoughts without judgment, and develop a greater sense of inner peace.
2. **Cognitive-Behavioral Therapy (CBT):** CBT is a therapeutic approach that focuses on identifying and challenging negative thought patterns and behaviors. It equips individuals with practical skills to reframe their thinking and develop healthier cognitive patterns.
3. **Emotional Expression:** Expressing emotions through writing, art, or conversation can be therapeutic. It allows us to process our feelings,

gain clarity, and reduce emotional tension. Journaling, for example, provides an outlet for self-reflection and emotional release.

4. **Social Connection:** Building and maintaining meaningful relationships is crucial for mental well-being. Social support provides a sense of belonging, reduces feelings of isolation, and offers a source of emotional comfort.
5. **Professional Help:** Seeking help from mental health professionals, such as therapists or counselors, can be a pivotal step in healing minds. These experts offer guidance, tools, and support tailored to individual needs.
6. **Stress Reduction Techniques:** Managing stress is essential for mental well-being. Techniques such as deep breathing, progressive muscle relaxation, and time management can help reduce stress levels and enhance resilience.
7. **Self-Compassion:** Self-compassion involves treating ourselves with the same kindness and understanding that we offer to others. It is the practice of self-acceptance and self-forgiveness, acknowledging that we are imperfect but worthy of love and care.
8. **Positive Psychology:** Positive psychology explores the cultivation of strengths, resilience, and happiness. It emphasizes focusing on strengths rather than weaknesses and fostering a positive outlook on life.

Personalizing Your Healing Journey

The journey to healing minds is deeply personal. What works for one person may not work for another, and that's perfectly normal. The key is to explore and experiment with different strategies to discover what resonates with you.

Here are some steps to personalize your healing journey:

1. **Self-Assessment:** Reflect on your current state of mental well-being. Identify areas of strength and areas where you would like to improve.
2. **Goal Setting:** Set realistic and achievable goals for your mental well-being. What specific aspects of your mental health would you like to enhance or address?
3. **Exploration:** Experiment with various strategies for mental well-being. Start with the ones that resonate with you the most, and be open to

trying new approaches.

4. **Consistency:** Consistency is key. Incorporate your chosen strategies into your daily or weekly routine to create lasting change.
5. **Self-Compassion:** Be patient and compassionate with yourself throughout your healing journey. Progress may be gradual, and setbacks are a natural part of growth.

Conclusion: Your Path to Healing Minds

Healing minds is a journey of self-discovery and self-care. It is a testament to our resilience and capacity for growth. As you explore the strategies for mental well-being, remember that you are not alone on this path. Seek support when needed, whether from friends, family, or mental health professionals.

The power to heal your mind lies within you. It is a journey of empowerment and transformation—one that leads to greater mental well-being, emotional balance, and a renewed sense of purpose.

As we delve into the specific mental health needs in the chapters to come, keep these strategies in mind. They are tools in your toolbox, ready to assist you on your journey of healing and thriving.

Your path to healing minds begins now.

Chapter 4

Breaking Barriers: Empowering Mental Health

In a world where mental health challenges persist, it is imperative that we break down the barriers that hinder access to support and empowerment.

Imagine a world where seeking help for mental health challenges is as natural as seeking medical assistance for a physical ailment. A world where individuals are empowered to prioritize their mental well-being without fear of judgment or discrimination. Such a world is not only possible but essential for the collective well-being of society. To bring this vision to fruition, we must engage in the vital work of breaking down the barriers that surround mental health.

The Silent Epidemic

Mental health challenges are often referred to as the silent epidemic, and for a good reason. While the impact of these challenges is widespread and profound, the silence and stigma surrounding them persist. Individuals often suffer in silence, fearing the judgment or misunderstanding of others.

This silence exacerbates the suffering, perpetuates stigma, and hinders access to vital support and treatment. It is essential to recognize that mental health challenges are not a sign of weakness but a part of the human experience. They affect individuals of all backgrounds, ages, and walks of life.

The Barriers to Mental Health Empowerment

The barriers that stand between individuals and mental health empowerment are multifaceted and complex. They include:

1. **Stigma:** Stigma remains one of the most significant barriers to seeking help for mental health challenges. It creates a culture of silence and shame, discouraging individuals from opening up about their struggles or seeking support.
2. **Lack of Awareness:** Many people lack awareness of mental health issues, available resources, and the importance of seeking help. This lack of knowledge can prevent early intervention and support.
3. **Access to Care:** Inequities in access to mental health care persist. Factors such as geographic location, socioeconomic status, and insurance coverage can limit access to treatment and support.

4. **Cultural and Social Barriers:** Cultural beliefs, social norms, and discrimination can create additional barriers for individuals from marginalized communities, making it more challenging to seek help.
5. **Mental Health Workforce Shortages:** Shortages of mental health professionals, particularly in underserved areas, can limit access to timely and appropriate care.

The Empowerment Imperative

Empowering mental health is not a luxury but a necessity. It is essential for individual well-being, community resilience, and societal progress. Empowerment in mental health involves:

1. **Raising Awareness:** Increasing awareness about mental health issues and the importance of seeking help is a fundamental step in empowerment. Education and open conversations reduce stigma and encourage early intervention.
2. **Promoting Access:** Ensuring equitable access to mental health care is imperative. This includes increasing the availability of mental health services, reducing financial barriers, and expanding telehealth options.
3. **Fostering Supportive Environments:** Creating environments where individuals feel safe and supported in discussing their mental health challenges is vital. This includes workplaces, educational institutions, and communities that prioritize mental well-being.
4. **Advocating for Policy Change:** Advocacy for policy changes that enhance mental health support and access to care is essential. This includes advocating for mental health parity laws and increased funding for mental health services.
5. **Cultural Competence:** Developing cultural competence among mental health professionals is crucial to address the unique needs of diverse populations effectively.

Breaking Down Stigma

Stigma surrounding mental health is a formidable barrier that must be dismantled. Stigma perpetuates silence, shame, and discrimination, making it difficult for individuals to seek help or open up about their struggles. Here are steps we can take to break down stigma:

1. **Education:** Educate yourself and others about mental health issues. Learn about common myths and misconceptions and challenge them with facts and empathy.
2. **Language Matters:** Be mindful of the language you use when discussing mental health. Avoid derogatory terms and stigmatizing language.
3. **Open Conversations:** Encourage open conversations about mental health with friends, family, and colleagues. Normalize discussions about emotions, stress, and well-being.
4. **Lead by Example:** Embrace vulnerability and authenticity in your own life. Share your mental health journey when appropriate to reduce stigma and create a culture of understanding.
5. **Support Others:** Be a source of support for those struggling with mental health challenges. Listen without judgment, offer assistance in finding resources, and promote a compassionate and understanding environment.

Access to Care

Access to mental health care is a fundamental right. To improve access:

1. **Advocate:** Advocate for policies that increase funding for mental health services and reduce financial barriers to care.
2. **Telehealth:** Explore telehealth options, which have become more widely available and accessible, particularly in response to the COVID-19 pandemic.
3. **Community Resources:** Seek out community mental health resources, such as support groups and nonprofit organizations, that provide affordable or free services.
4. **Insurance:** Advocate for mental health parity laws that ensure equal coverage for mental health services by insurance providers.

Cultural Competence

Cultural competence is vital in addressing the diverse needs of individuals seeking mental health support. It involves understanding and respecting the cultural, linguistic, and social backgrounds of individuals:

1. **Cultural Training:** Mental health professionals should receive training in cultural competence to provide culturally sensitive care.
2. **Community Partnerships:** Collaborate with community organizations that serve specific cultural or ethnic groups to enhance outreach and support.
3. **Language Access:** Ensure that language services, such as interpreters, are available for individuals who speak languages other than English.

Advocacy for Change

Advocacy plays a critical role in breaking down barriers to mental health empowerment. Consider engaging in advocacy efforts that promote mental health awareness and support:

1. **Mental Health Organizations:** Join or support organizations dedicated to mental health advocacy and awareness, such as the National Alliance on Mental Illness (NAMI) or Mental Health America (MHA).
2. **Legislative Advocacy:** Participate in legislative advocacy efforts that aim to improve mental health policies and increase funding for mental health services.

Conclusion: The Power of Empowerment

Breaking down barriers to mental health empowerment is a collective endeavor. It requires a commitment to raising awareness, reducing stigma, and advocating for change. Empowering mental health is not only a moral imperative but also an investment in the well-being and resilience of individuals and communities.

As we delve into the specific mental health needs in the chapters to come, keep in mind the importance of breaking down barriers and promoting access to support. Together, we can create a world where mental health is prioritized, stigma is eradicated, and every individual has the opportunity to thrive.

The journey to empower mental health starts now.

Chapter 5

From Struggle to Strength: Mastering Mental Health Needs

Within every struggle lies the potential for growth, resilience, and mastery of our mental health needs.

Life is a series of challenges and triumphs, and nowhere is this more evident than in our mental health journey. From the depths of despair to the heights of well-being, our struggles with mental health needs shape our character and resilience. This chapter explores the transformative power of mastering our mental health needs, recognizing that within the crucible of adversity lies the potential for strength and growth.

The Complexity of Mental Health Needs

Mental health needs are as diverse as the individuals who experience them. They encompass a broad range of challenges, from anxiety and depression to trauma and addiction. Each person's journey with mental health is unique, influenced by genetics, environment, life experiences, and personal resilience.

It's crucial to acknowledge that mental health needs are not a sign of weakness but a natural part of the human experience. We all face moments of emotional distress, and seeking support and strategies to master these needs is a testament to our strength and self-awareness.

The Path from Struggle to Strength

The journey from struggle to strength in managing mental health needs is a dynamic process. It involves self-discovery, self-compassion, and the cultivation of coping strategies. Here are the key steps on this transformative path:

1. **Self-Awareness:** The first step is self-awareness—recognizing and acknowledging your mental health needs. This involves identifying patterns, triggers, and the impact of these needs on your life.
2. **Acceptance:** Acceptance is the act of embracing your mental health needs without judgment. It is acknowledging that these needs are a part of who you are and that seeking help is a courageous choice.
3. **Seeking Support:** Seeking support is a pivotal step. Whether through friends, family, or mental health professionals, reaching out for assistance can provide invaluable guidance and resources.

4. **Developing Coping Strategies:** Coping strategies are tools and techniques that empower you to manage your mental health needs. These strategies may include mindfulness, therapy, medication, exercise, or creative expression.
5. **Resilience Building:** Resilience is the ability to bounce back from adversity. Building resilience involves developing emotional strength, adaptability, and the capacity to thrive in the face of challenges.
6. **Self-Care:** Self-care is an essential component of mastering mental health needs. It involves prioritizing activities and practices that promote well-being and reduce stress.
7. **Creating a Supportive Environment:** Surrounding yourself with a supportive network of friends and loved ones can significantly impact your ability to master your mental health needs.

Embracing Vulnerability

Vulnerability is often seen as a weakness, but it is a profound source of strength in the context of mental health needs. Embracing vulnerability means allowing yourself to be authentic and open about your struggles. It means reaching out for help when needed, even when it feels uncomfortable.

Consider this: when you open up about your mental health needs, you not only invite support but also inspire others to do the same. You break down the walls of stigma and create a culture of understanding and empathy. Vulnerability is the key to connection, and connection is a powerful source of healing.

The Transformative Power of Resilience

Resilience is the ability to withstand and rebound from adversity. It is not an inherent trait but a skill that can be cultivated and strengthened. Building resilience is essential in mastering mental health needs because it equips you to navigate the inevitable challenges of life.

Resilience involves:

1. **Emotional Regulation:** The capacity to manage and regulate your emotions effectively, reducing the impact of stress and emotional turmoil.
2. **Problem-Solving:** Developing problem-solving skills to address the challenges and triggers that contribute to your mental health needs.

3. **Adaptability:** The ability to adapt to change and uncertainty, which are inherent aspects of life.
4. **Social Support:** Building and maintaining supportive relationships that serve as a source of comfort and understanding.
5. **Positive Outlook:** Cultivating a positive outlook on life, even in the face of difficulties, by focusing on strengths and opportunities.

Turning Struggles into Opportunities

Every struggle with mental health needs presents an opportunity for growth, self-discovery, and resilience. Instead of viewing these challenges as obstacles, consider them as moments of transformation. They are the catalysts for self-improvement, self-compassion, and personal empowerment.

1. **Self-Improvement:** The journey of mastering mental health needs often involves self-improvement. It may lead you to develop new skills, adopt healthier habits, and enhance your emotional intelligence.
2. **Self-Compassion:** Struggles with mental health needs can teach you the value of self-compassion. It is the practice of treating yourself with kindness, forgiveness, and understanding, even in the midst of challenges.
3. **Personal Empowerment:** Mastery of mental health needs is a form of personal empowerment. It involves taking control of your well-being, advocating for your needs, and making choices that prioritize your mental health.

Supportive Networks and Communities

Creating and nurturing supportive networks and communities is a fundamental aspect of mastering mental health needs. These networks can include friends, family, support groups, and mental health professionals. They provide a safety net of understanding and assistance during difficult times.

Conclusion: The Triumph of Strength

In mastering mental health needs, we discover the triumph of strength within ourselves. It is the strength to acknowledge our struggles, seek help when needed, and cultivate resilience. It is the strength to embrace vulnerability and authenticity, breaking down the walls of stigma.

As we delve into the specific mental health needs in the chapters to come, remember that your struggles can be the source of your greatest strength. They are the crucible in which resilience is forged, and they hold the potential for transformation and growth.

Your journey from struggle to strength in mastering mental health needs starts now.

Chapter 6

Resilience: Your Guide to Mental Wellness

In the face of life's storms, resilience is the anchor that keeps us grounded and the sail that propels us forward toward mental wellness.

Life is full of challenges, uncertainties, and moments of adversity. These experiences can take a toll on our mental well-being, leading to stress, anxiety, and other mental health needs. In such times, resilience becomes our guiding light—a powerful force that helps us navigate the storms of life and find our way to mental wellness.

The Essence of Resilience

Resilience is not a passive trait but an active skill an art that can be cultivated and strengthened. It is the ability to bounce back from adversity, adapt to change, and thrive in the face of challenges. Resilience empowers us to overcome setbacks, persevere through difficulties, and maintain our mental wellness.

Resilience encompasses various aspects of our lives, including emotional, cognitive, social, and physical well-being. It is not a fixed attribute but a dynamic quality that evolves as we face and conquer life's challenges.

The Pillars of Resilience

Resilience is built upon several foundational pillars, each contributing to our ability to withstand adversity and nurture our mental wellness:

1. **Emotional Regulation:** Emotional regulation is the capacity to manage and control our emotions effectively. It involves recognizing and expressing emotions in a healthy and constructive way.
2. **Self-Awareness:** Self-awareness is the foundation of resilience. It involves understanding our thoughts, feelings, and behaviors and their impact on our mental well-being.
3. **Adaptability:** Adaptability is the ability to adjust to change and uncertainty. It enables us to navigate transitions and challenges with flexibility and confidence.
4. **Problem-Solving:** Problem-solving skills help us identify and address the root causes of our challenges. They empower us to find solutions and make constructive choices.

5. **Social Support:** Building and maintaining supportive relationships is vital for resilience. Social support provides a safety net of understanding and assistance during difficult times.
6. **Positive Outlook:** A positive outlook on life is a cornerstone of resilience. It involves focusing on strengths, opportunities, and possibilities, even in the face of adversity.

Building Resilience for Mental Wellness

Building resilience is an ongoing journey—a commitment to nurturing our mental wellness and fortifying our inner strength. Here are key strategies to cultivate resilience in your life:

1. **Embrace Emotional Awareness:** Cultivate emotional awareness by paying attention to your feelings and their triggers. Practice labeling your emotions and expressing them in healthy ways, such as journaling or talking to a trusted friend.
2. **Develop Stress-Reduction Techniques:** Learn stress-reduction techniques, such as deep breathing, progressive muscle relaxation, and mindfulness meditation. These practices help reduce the physiological effects of stress on your body and mind.
3. **Foster a Growth Mindset:** Embrace a growth mindset by viewing challenges as opportunities for growth and learning. Challenge negative self-talk and replace it with self-compassion and optimism.
4. **Maintain Supportive Relationships:** Build and nurture supportive relationships with friends and loved ones. Seek out individuals who provide emotional support, understanding, and encouragement.
5. **Seek Professional Help When Needed:** Don't hesitate to seek professional help from therapists or counselors if you are facing significant mental health challenges. They can provide guidance, strategies, and support tailored to your needs.
6. **Practice Self-Care:** Prioritize self-care activities that promote mental wellness, such as regular exercise, adequate sleep, a balanced diet, and engaging in hobbies and activities you enjoy.
7. **Develop Problem-Solving Skills:** Enhance your problem-solving skills by breaking down challenges into manageable steps,

brainstorming solutions, and taking action to address them.

8. **Cultivate Resilient Thinking:** Challenge negative and catastrophic thinking patterns. Replace them with resilient thinking that acknowledges difficulties while also recognizing your ability to cope and adapt.

Resilience in Action

To illustrate the power of resilience, let's consider a scenario:

Imagine you are facing a significant life change, such as a job loss. This situation can trigger various emotions, including stress, anxiety, and uncertainty. However, with resilience, you can respond effectively:

1. **Emotional Regulation:** You recognize your feelings of anxiety and stress. Instead of letting them overwhelm you, you use mindfulness techniques to calm your mind and reduce emotional intensity.
2. **Adaptability:** You view the job loss as an opportunity for personal and professional growth. You start exploring new career paths and acquiring new skills, adapting to the change with optimism.
3. **Problem-Solving:** You develop a plan to address your financial needs during the transition period. This includes creating a budget, exploring alternative income sources, and seeking out job opportunities.
4. **Social Support:** You reach out to friends and family for emotional support. Their encouragement and understanding provide a sense of comfort and reassurance.
5. **Positive Outlook:** You maintain a positive outlook, believing in your ability to navigate this challenging period successfully. You focus on the possibilities that lie ahead.

Conclusion: Resilience as a Lifelong Journey

Resilience is not a destination but a lifelong journey. It is a skill that can be honed and developed throughout our lives. By cultivating resilience, we empower ourselves to navigate the challenges of life with grace and mental wellness.

As we explore specific mental health needs in the chapters to come, keep in mind that resilience is the foundation upon which we can build our capacity to thrive. It is the anchor that keeps us grounded and the sail that propels us forward toward mental wellness.

Your journey to resilience and mental wellness starts now.

Chapter 7

Mindful Living: Unlocking Mental Health Potential

In the art of mindfulness, we discover the power of the present moment—a gateway to unlocking our mental health potential.

In the fast-paced whirlwind of modern life, our minds often wander between regrets about the past and worries about the future. We rarely pause to fully experience the present moment. Yet, within the realm of mindfulness, we find a profound key to unlocking our mental health potential.

The Essence of Mindfulness

Mindfulness is a way of being—of fully engaging with the present moment without judgment. It is the practice of paying deliberate attention to our thoughts, feelings, sensations, and the environment around us. At its core, mindfulness is about cultivating awareness and presence in our daily lives.

Mindfulness does not involve emptying the mind or achieving a state of perpetual bliss. Instead, it invites us to embrace the richness of our experiences, including discomfort and challenges. It is through this awareness that we can unlock our mental health potential.

The Benefits of Mindfulness for Mental Health

Mindfulness is not a new-age fad; it is a scientifically validated practice with a myriad of benefits for mental health. These benefits extend to individuals of all backgrounds and ages. Here are some ways in which mindfulness can enhance mental well-being:

1. **Stress Reduction:** Mindfulness reduces the physiological and psychological effects of stress, promoting a sense of calm and resilience.
2. **Emotional Regulation:** Mindfulness enhances emotional regulation skills, enabling individuals to respond to emotions in a balanced and constructive way.
3. **Improved Focus:** Regular mindfulness practice sharpens concentration and attention, making it easier to stay engaged in tasks and reduce distractibility.
4. **Reduced Anxiety:** Mindfulness reduces symptoms of anxiety disorders, helping individuals manage worry and intrusive thoughts.

5. **Enhanced Self-Awareness:** Through mindfulness, individuals gain deeper insights into their thoughts, feelings, and behaviors, fostering self-awareness and personal growth.
6. **Pain Management:** Mindfulness is effective in pain management, providing individuals with tools to cope with physical and emotional pain.
7. **Enhanced Well-Being:** Mindfulness practices increase overall well-being by promoting positive emotions, life satisfaction, and a sense of purpose.

The Practice of Mindfulness

Mindfulness is not limited to formal meditation; it can be integrated into every aspect of life. Here are some key mindfulness practices to unlock your mental health potential:

1. **Mindful Breathing:** Take a few moments each day to focus on your breath. Pay attention to the sensations of inhaling and exhaling. When your mind wanders, gently bring your attention back to your breath.
2. **Body Scan:** Perform a body scan by directing your attention to different parts of your body, starting from your toes and moving up to your head. Notice any sensations or tension without judgment.
3. **Mindful Eating:** Savor your meals by eating slowly and paying attention to the taste, texture, and aroma of your food. Avoid distractions, such as phones or television, during meals.
4. **Mindful Walking:** While walking, bring your attention to the sensation of each step—the contact of your foot with the ground, the movement of your legs, and the rhythm of your breath.
5. **Meditation:** Set aside time for formal meditation. Start with short sessions and gradually extend the duration as you become more comfortable. Guided meditation apps and videos can be helpful for beginners.
6. **Mindful Listening:** Practice active listening by fully engaging with the speaker without interrupting or formulating a response in your mind. Listen with openness and empathy.

Mindfulness in Daily Life

Beyond formal practices, mindfulness can be integrated into your daily routines:

1. **Morning Rituals:** Begin your day mindfully by setting intentions and taking a few moments for deep breathing or a short meditation.
2. **Mindful Movement:** Engage in mindful movement practices which combine physical activity with mindfulness.
3. **Tech-Free Time:** Dedicate tech-free moments during your day to unplug from screens and connect with your surroundings.
4. **Mindful Communication:** Practice mindful communication by being fully present in your interactions, whether with family, friends, or colleagues.
5. **Mindful Pauses:** Throughout your day, take mindful pauses to breathe deeply and ground yourself in the present moment.

Overcoming Common Challenges

While mindfulness offers numerous benefits, it's essential to acknowledge common challenges that may arise:

1. **Restlessness:** It's normal for the mind to wander during mindfulness practice. Gently guide your focus back to the present when this happens.
2. **Impatience:** Cultivating mindfulness takes time and practice. Be patient with yourself and embrace imperfection.
3. **Resistance:** Resistance may arise when facing uncomfortable emotions or sensations. Allow these experiences to be part of your mindfulness practice.
4. **Inconsistency:** Consistency is key to reaping the benefits of mindfulness. Establish a routine that works for you and commit to regular practice.

Unlocking Your Mental Health Potential

Unlocking your mental health potential through mindfulness is a journey of self-discovery and self-compassion. As you engage in mindfulness practices, you may notice shifts in your mental well-being and resilience. Here's how mindfulness unlocks your mental health potential:

1. **Enhanced Awareness:** Mindfulness heightens your awareness of thoughts and emotions, allowing you to respond to them consciously rather than reactively.
2. **Emotional Regulation:** Through mindfulness, you develop the ability to manage and regulate your emotions effectively.
3. **Reduced Stress:** Mindfulness reduces stress by promoting relaxation and reducing the physiological and psychological impacts of stress.
4. **Improved Focus:** Your ability to stay present and focused is strengthened, enhancing your cognitive function.
5. **Enhanced Well-Being:** Overall well-being is elevated as you cultivate positive emotions, life satisfaction, and a sense of purpose.

Conclusion: The Present Moment as Your Ally

Mindful living is a practice of embracing the present moment as your ally in nurturing mental wellness. In the midst of life's challenges, it offers a sanctuary of awareness, resilience, and well-being.

As we explore specific mental health needs in the chapters to come, remember that mindfulness is a tool that can enhance your mental health potential. It is a lifelong journey that unfolds with each breath, each step, and each moment of presence.

Your path to unlocking your mental health potential through mindful living starts now.

Chapter 8

Rising Above: A Journey to Mental Well-Being

In the tapestry of our lives, the thread of mental well-being weaves a vibrant and resilient fabric.

Life's journey is often marked by twists and turns, challenges, and triumphs. Amidst this ever-changing landscape, mental well-being is the compass that guides us—a beacon of light that illuminates the path to a fulfilling and balanced life. This chapter explores the profound journey to mental well-being, emphasizing that it is within our reach, regardless of the challenges we face.

The Landscape of Mental Well-Being

Mental well-being encompasses a broad spectrum of experiences, emotions, and states of mind. It is not the absence of challenges or negative emotions but the ability to navigate them with resilience and a sense of equilibrium.

Mental well-being involves:

1. **Emotional Resilience:** The capacity to bounce back from setbacks, cope with stress, and adapt to change.
2. **Positive Emotions:** Experiencing joy, gratitude, contentment, and other positive emotions that enhance our quality of life.
3. **Self-Awareness:** Understanding our thoughts, feelings, and behaviors and their impact on our well-being.
4. **Healthy Relationships:** Building and nurturing supportive relationships that contribute to our emotional and psychological growth.
5. **Purpose and Meaning:** Discovering a sense of purpose and meaning in our lives that drives our actions and fuels our well-being.

The Journey to Mental Well-Being

The journey to mental well-being is a lifelong process a dynamic and evolving tapestry that we weave with intention and care. While the path may vary for each individual, there are essential elements that define this journey:

1. **Self-Exploration:** The journey begins with self-exploration—a deep dive into your thoughts, emotions, values, and beliefs. It involves

reflecting on your life experiences and understanding how they have shaped your mental well-being.

2. **Emotional Resilience:** Building emotional resilience is a crucial component of the journey. It involves developing the capacity to manage stress, regulate emotions, and bounce back from adversity.
3. **Positive Psychology:** Embracing positive psychology principles allows you to cultivate positive emotions, strengths, and a sense of purpose. It's about shifting your focus from what's wrong to what's right in your life.
4. **Relationship Building:** Building and nurturing healthy relationships is essential for mental well-being. Supportive connections with friends, family, and community can provide a safety net of understanding and assistance during difficult times.
5. **Self-Care:** Prioritizing self-care activities that promote physical, emotional, and mental well-being is fundamental. Self-care includes practices such as exercise, relaxation, mindfulness, and hobbies that bring joy.
6. **Meaning and Purpose:** Seeking meaning and purpose is a transformative aspect of the journey. It involves identifying your values and aligning your actions with your deepest aspirations.
7. **Resilience and Coping:** Developing coping strategies and resilience skills equips you to navigate life's challenges effectively. It's about finding constructive ways to respond to stress and adversity.

The Role of Positive Psychology

Positive psychology is a guiding light on the journey to mental well-being. It emphasizes the cultivation of strengths, resilience, and happiness. Here's how positive psychology contributes to the journey:

1. **Strengths-Based Approach:** Positive psychology encourages a strengths-based approach, focusing on what individuals do well and their unique qualities.
2. **Gratitude:** Gratitude is a cornerstone of positive psychology. Practicing gratitude fosters a sense of contentment and appreciation for the present moment.

3. **Optimism:** Positive psychology promotes optimism—a positive outlook on life that sees challenges as opportunities for growth.
4. **Mindfulness:** Mindfulness practices are central to positive psychology, fostering awareness, presence, and emotional regulation.
5. **Flow:** The concept of flow, or being fully immersed in an activity, is another key element of positive psychology that enhances well-being.

The Transformative Power of Resilience

Resilience is a fundamental aspect of mental well-being. It is the ability to withstand adversity, adapt to change, and bounce back from setbacks. Resilience allows us to face life's challenges with courage and resourcefulness.

Building resilience involves:

1. **Emotional Regulation:** The ability to manage and regulate emotions effectively, reducing the impact of stress and emotional turmoil.
2. **Problem-Solving:** Developing problem-solving skills to address the challenges and triggers that affect our mental well-being.
3. **Social Support:** Building and maintaining supportive relationships that serve as a source of comfort and understanding.
4. **Positive Outlook:** Cultivating a positive outlook on life, even in the face of difficulties, by focusing on strengths and opportunities.

The Role of Self-Care

Self-care is a cornerstone of mental well-being. It is the practice of prioritizing activities and practices that promote well-being and reduce stress. Self-care includes:

1. **Physical Health:** Engaging in regular physical activity, maintaining a balanced diet, and getting adequate sleep.
2. **Emotional Health:** Practicing emotional regulation and self-compassion, seeking therapy when needed, and expressing emotions constructively.
3. **Mindfulness and Relaxation:** Incorporating mindfulness, meditation, and relaxation techniques into your daily routine.
4. **Social Connections:** Nurturing supportive relationships with friends and loved ones and seeking social support when facing challenges.

5. **Creativity and Hobbies:** Engaging in creative activities and hobbies that bring joy and relaxation.

Discovering Meaning and Purpose

One of the most transformative aspects of the journey to mental well-being is discovering meaning and purpose in your life. It involves:

1. **Values Exploration:** Identifying your core values what truly matters to you in life.
2. **Goal Setting:** Setting meaningful goals aligned with your values and aspirations.
3. **Contributing to Others:** Finding ways to contribute to the well-being of others and the community, which enhances your sense of purpose.

Conclusion: Your Journey to Mental Well-Being

The journey to mental well-being is a dynamic and evolving process that requires intention, self-compassion, and resilience. It is a tapestry woven from self-exploration, emotional resilience, positive psychology, relationships, self-care, and a sense of meaning and purpose.

As we delve into the specific mental health needs in the chapters to come, remember that the journey to mental well-being is within your reach. It is a journey of self-discovery, growth, and resilience—a journey that allows you to rise above challenges and embrace the fullness of life.

Your journey to mental well-being starts now.

Chapter 9

Thriving in Turbulent Times: Your Mental Health Roadmap

In the midst of life's storms, your mental health roadmap becomes your guiding star, leading you toward a place of thriving.

Life is an ever-changing journey, often marked by unpredictability, challenges, and moments of turbulence. These turbulent times can put a strain on our mental health, but with a well-constructed mental health roadmap, we can through adversity and not just survive but thrive. In this chapter, we explore the essential components of your mental health roadmap and how to utilize it effectively.

Understanding Turbulent Times

Turbulent times are characterized by external stressors or internal struggles that can disrupt our sense of well-being. They can take various forms, such as:

1. **External Challenges:** These include life events such as financial difficulties, job loss, relationship problems, or the loss of a loved one.
2. **Internal Struggles:** Internal turbulence can arise from mental health conditions like anxiety, depression, or trauma, as well as from negative thought patterns and emotional distress.
3. **Global and Societal Events:** Events like natural disasters, economic crises, or pandemics can create widespread turbulence that affects individuals on a collective level.

The Mental Health Roadmap

Your mental health roadmap is a personalized and flexible plan that equips you to navigate turbulent times effectively. It serves as your guiding star, helping you find your way back to mental well-being. Here are the key components:

1. **Self-Awareness:** The foundation of your roadmap is self-awareness. This involves recognizing your emotions, thoughts, and triggers. Self-awareness allows you to identify when you are experiencing turbulence and the specific mental health needs that arise.
2. **Resilience Building:** Building resilience is crucial for thriving in turbulent times. Resilience involves developing emotional strength,

adaptability, and the capacity to bounce back from adversity.

3. **Support System:** Your roadmap includes a support system consisting of friends, family, mentors, or mental health professionals who can provide assistance, guidance, and understanding during difficult times.
4. **Coping Strategies:** Develop a repertoire of coping strategies that suit your unique needs. These strategies may include mindfulness, relaxation techniques, exercise, creative outlets, or therapy.
5. **Self-Care:** Prioritize self-care activities that promote physical, emotional, and mental well-being. Self-care provides a buffer against the stressors of turbulent times.
6. **Mindfulness:** Incorporate mindfulness practices into your daily routine. Mindfulness enhances your ability to stay present and manage stress effectively.
7. **Adaptability:** Cultivate adaptability as a mindset. Being open to change and resilient in the face of uncertainty is a valuable skill.
8. **Positive Psychology:** Embrace positive psychology principles, focusing on strengths, optimism, gratitude, and positive emotions as tools for thriving.

Self-Awareness: The Compass of Your Roadmap

Self-awareness is the compass of your mental health roadmap. It allows you to navigate turbulent times by understanding your emotional landscape, thought patterns, and triggers. Here's how to cultivate self-awareness:

1. **Emotion Recognition:** Practice recognizing and labeling your emotions. Keep a journal to track your emotional experiences and identify patterns.
2. **Mindful Self-Reflection:** Engage in mindful self-reflection by setting aside time each day to check in with yourself. Ask yourself how you are feeling emotionally, mentally, and physically.
3. **Thought Monitoring:** Pay attention to your thought patterns. Are they predominantly negative or positive? Are they helpful or unhelpful? Identifying negative thought patterns allows you to challenge and reframe them.
4. **Trigger Awareness:** Be mindful of the situations, people, or

circumstances that trigger emotional distress or turbulence. Recognizing these triggers can help you develop strategies to manage them.

Building Resilience: Your Armor in Turbulence

Resilience is your armor in turbulent times. It equips you to withstand adversity and bounce back from setbacks. Here's how to build resilience:

1. **Emotional Regulation:** Develop emotional regulation skills to manage intense emotions effectively. Techniques like deep breathing, progressive muscle relaxation, and mindfulness can help.
2. **Problem-Solving:** Enhance your problem-solving skills to address the challenges and stressors you encounter. Break down problems into manageable steps and take proactive measures.
3. **Social Support:** Lean on your support system during turbulent times. Share your challenges and emotions with trusted friends or family members who can provide comfort and understanding.
4. **Positive Outlook:** Cultivate a positive outlook on life by focusing on your strengths, opportunities, and the potential for growth even in difficult circumstances.

The Role of Support System

Your support system is a critical element of your mental health roadmap. These are the individuals who offer understanding, empathy, and assistance when you need it most. Consider the following when building your support system:

1. **Identify Key Supporters:** Identify friends, family members, mentors, or mental health professionals who can provide support during turbulent times.
2. **Communication:** Communicate your needs and feelings openly with your support system. Let them know how they can best assist you.
3. **Boundaries:** Establish boundaries to protect your mental well-being. Communicate your boundaries clearly and assertively to prevent overwhelm.
4. **Reach Out:** Don't hesitate to reach out to your support system when facing turbulence. Sharing your experiences can alleviate emotional

burdens and provide relief.

Coping Strategies: Tools in Your Toolbox

Your mental health roadmap includes coping strategies that serve as tools in your toolbox for managing turbulent times. Explore and practice a variety of coping mechanisms to determine what works best for you:

1. **Mindfulness and Relaxation:** Engage in mindfulness meditation, deep breathing exercises, or progressive muscle relaxation to reduce stress and promote emotional regulation.
2. **Exercise:** Physical activity can be a powerful tool for managing emotions and promoting mental well-being. Find an exercise routine that you enjoy and can commit to.
3. **Creative Expression:** Engage in creative outlets like art, writing, music, or dance to express your emotions and find solace.
4. **Therapy:** Consider seeking therapy or counseling from a mental health professional trained to provide support and guidance during challenging times.
5. **Positive Activities:** Engage in activities that bring you joy and fulfillment. This could include spending time with loved ones, pursuing hobbies, or volunteering.

Self-Care: Your Daily Rituals

Self-care is the foundation of your mental health roadmap. It involves daily rituals and practices that prioritize your well-being. Here's how to establish a self-care routine:

1. **Assess Your Needs:** Identify your physical, emotional, and mental needs. What activities or practices promote well-being for you?
2. **Create a Routine:** Establish a daily self-care routine that incorporates activities that nourish your mind, body, and soul.
3. **Prioritize Rest:** Ensure you get enough sleep and rest to rejuvenate your body and mind.
4. **Healthy Diet:** Maintain a balanced diet that supports your physical and mental health.
5. **Exercise:** Incorporate regular physical activity into your routine to

release endorphins and reduce stress.

Chapter 10

Reclaiming Joy: Transforming Mental Health Challenges

In the depths of mental health challenges, lies the potential for transformation, growth, and the rediscovery of joy.

Throughout this journey into the realm of mental health, we have explored the intricate landscape of emotions, resilience, self-awareness, and the tools at our disposal for navigating the turbulent seas of life. In this final chapter, we delve into the transformative power that arises from facing mental health challenges head-on and how we can reclaim joy in the process.

The Nature of Mental Health Challenges

Mental health challenges can encompass a wide range of experiences, from common conditions like anxiety and depression to more complex issues such as trauma or addiction. These challenges can disrupt our lives, affecting our relationships, work, and overall well-being.

However, it's important to recognize that mental health challenges do not define us. They are a part of our journey, not the entirety of it. Just as storms pass, mental health challenges can be navigated, and we can emerge from them stronger and wiser.

The Potential for Transformation

In the midst of mental health challenges, there exists a profound potential for transformation. It is within the crucible of struggle that we can discover hidden strengths, gain self-awareness, and ultimately transform ourselves. Here are some ways in which transformation can occur:

1. **Self-Discovery:** Mental health challenges often prompt deep self-reflection. We may uncover aspects of ourselves we never knew existed or gain insights into long-standing patterns.
2. **Empathy:** Going through mental health challenges can cultivate empathy and compassion for others facing similar struggles. We become better equipped to support and understand one another.
3. **Resilience:** Surviving mental health challenges builds resilience. We learn that we can endure, adapt, and grow stronger even in the face of adversity.

4. **Reevaluation of Priorities:** Challenges force us to reassess our priorities. We may reprioritize what truly matters in life, leading to greater fulfillment and purpose.
5. **Increased Self-Care:** Mental health challenges often necessitate an emphasis on self-care. We become more attuned to our needs and prioritize practices that promote well-being.

The Role of Support

Support is invaluable when navigating mental health challenges. Whether from friends, family, or mental health professionals, support provides a lifeline during difficult times. Here's how to harness the power of support:

1. **Reach Out:** Don't hesitate to reach out to your support network. Share your experiences and emotions, as talking about your challenges can provide relief.
2. **Therapy:** Consider therapy or counseling from a mental health professional who can provide guidance and strategies tailored to your needs.
3. **Peer Support:** Peer support groups or online communities can be a source of understanding and connection with others who have faced similar challenges.
4. **Communication:** Be open and honest in your communication with your support system. Let them know how they can assist you effectively.

Cultivating Resilience

Resilience is a vital asset when confronting mental health challenges. It enables us to adapt, persevere, and emerge stronger. Here are some ways to cultivate resilience:

1. **Emotional Regulation:** Develop emotional regulation skills to manage the intense emotions that often accompany mental health challenges.
2. **Self-Compassion:** Practice self-compassion by treating yourself with the same kindness and understanding you would offer to a friend.
3. **Positive Coping Mechanisms:** Build a repertoire of positive coping

mechanisms, such as mindfulness, relaxation techniques, or creative outlets.

4. **Growth Mindset:** Embrace a growth mindset that views challenges as opportunities for personal development and learning.
5. **Social Support:** Lean on your support system during challenging times. Seek understanding and encouragement from friends, family, or support groups.

Rediscovering Joy

Amidst mental health challenges, it may seem that joy has faded into the background. However, joy is not lost but temporarily obscured. Here are strategies to rediscover and nurture joy:

1. **Gratitude Practice:** Cultivate gratitude by focusing on the positive aspects of life, no matter how small. Create a daily gratitude journal to capture moments of joy.
2. **Engage in Activities You Love:** Reconnect with hobbies, interests, or activities that bring you joy and fulfillment.
3. **Mindfulness:** Practice mindfulness to savor the present moment and find joy in simple pleasures.
4. **Seek Pleasure:** Make a deliberate effort to seek out activities that bring you pleasure and enjoyment.
5. **Connect with Loved Ones:** Spend time with loved ones who bring joy and positivity into your life.

The Path to Healing

Healing from mental health challenges is not linear, and it may involve setbacks along the way. It's essential to be patient with yourself and acknowledge that healing is a journey. Here are steps to embrace the path to healing:

1. **Acceptance:** Accept that mental health challenges are a part of your journey, not a reflection of your worth.
2. **Professional Help:** Seek professional help if needed. Therapists and counselors can provide guidance and strategies tailored to your situation.
3. **Self-Compassion:** Treat yourself with compassion and kindness.

Avoid self-criticism and negative self-talk.

4. **Healthy Lifestyle:** Prioritize a healthy lifestyle that includes regular exercise, a balanced diet, and adequate sleep.
5. **Support System:** Lean on your support system for understanding, empathy, and assistance when necessary.

Conclusion: Reclaiming Joy

In the tapestry of our lives, mental health challenges may represent moments of darkness, but they do not define the entirety of our story. By embracing these challenges, seeking support, cultivating resilience, and nurturing joy, we have the power to transform ourselves and reclaim the joy that is our birthright.

Remember that you are not alone on this journey. Reach out to your support system, seek professional help if needed, and never underestimate the resilience of the human spirit. Your capacity for transformation, growth, and joy is boundless, and the path to reclaiming it starts now.

May your journey be filled with healing, rediscovery, and the joy that emerges from within.

Chapter 11

A Call to Action for Mental Health

The time has come to stand together and champion mental health as a collective cause, fostering understanding, support, and change.

As we conclude this journey through the intricate landscape of mental health, we stand at a pivotal moment in history. The conversations surrounding mental health have evolved, breaking the silence and stigma that have shrouded it for far too long. Yet, our work is far from over. We are called upon to take action, not just as individuals but as a global community, to drive change, compassion, and progress in the realm of mental health.

The Global Mental Health Challenge

Mental health challenges know no borders, affecting people of all ages, backgrounds, and walks of life. They are not limited to a particular region or demographic but touch every corner of our world. The statistics are staggering millions of lives are impacted by mental health conditions, and the consequences ripple through families, communities, and societies.

The global mental health challenge is not an isolated issue; it is intertwined with numerous societal factors, including access to healthcare, social support systems, economic disparities, and cultural attitudes. To address this challenge effectively, we must recognize it as a shared responsibility that calls for collective action.

Breaking the Silence

One of the most critical steps in addressing mental health is breaking the silence that has perpetuated stigma and discrimination. By speaking openly about our own experiences and supporting others in doing the same, we can dispel myths and misconceptions surrounding mental health conditions.

Breaking the silence means:

1. **Sharing Our Stories:** By sharing our personal stories, we can help others understand the reality of living with mental health challenges. We can inspire hope and foster empathy.
2. **Championing Vulnerability:** Vulnerability is not a sign of weakness but a demonstration of strength. By embracing vulnerability, we

encourage others to do the same.

3. **Creating Safe Spaces:** Establishing safe spaces where individuals can share their experiences without judgment is essential. These spaces foster understanding and support.

Fostering Understanding and Empathy

Understanding is the foundation upon which empathy is built. To foster understanding, we must educate ourselves and others about mental health, dispel myths, and promote accurate information. This understanding leads to empathy, which forms the basis of compassionate action.

Fostering understanding and empathy involves:

1. **Educational Initiatives:** Supporting educational programs that teach individuals about mental health, its prevalence, and the importance of seeking help when needed.
2. **Media Responsibility:** Encouraging responsible media portrayals of mental health issues and advocating for accurate and sensitive representation.
3. **Supporting Loved Ones:** Listening and supporting loved ones who may be facing mental health challenges, offering a helping hand, and encouraging them to seek professional help if necessary.
4. **Reducing Discrimination:** Standing against discrimination and advocating for policies and practices that promote equal treatment for individuals with mental health conditions.

Access to Care and Resources

Access to mental healthcare and resources is a fundamental right. It should not be determined by geographical location, socio-economic status, or other disparities. To ensure that everyone can access the care and resources they need, we must advocate for change at all levels of society.

Improving access to care involves:

1. **Policy Advocacy:** Advocating for policies that prioritize mental health, including increased funding for mental healthcare services and improved insurance coverage.
2. **Reducing Barriers:** Identifying and reducing barriers that prevent

individuals from seeking help, such as stigma, cost, or lack of available services.

3. **Promoting Early Intervention:** Emphasizing the importance of early intervention and prevention efforts to address mental health challenges before they escalate.
4. **Supportive Communities:** Creating communities that offer a network of support, including peer support groups, crisis hotlines, and online resources.

Advocacy and Activism

Advocacy and activism are powerful tools for driving change in the mental health landscape. As individuals and communities, we have the ability to raise our voices, demand action, and hold institutions accountable for their response to mental health needs.

Advocacy and activism encompass:

1. **Advocacy Organizations:** Supporting and engaging with organizations dedicated to mental health advocacy, research, and awareness.
2. **Legislative Action:** Participating in efforts to influence legislation and policy changes that benefit mental health care and access.
3. **Community Initiatives:** Initiating community-based projects and initiatives that promote mental health awareness and support.
4. **Media and Awareness Campaigns:** Participating in and promoting mental health awareness campaigns and events that reduce stigma and raise public awareness.

Supporting the Vulnerable

Mental health challenges can affect vulnerable populations disproportionately. This includes individuals facing discrimination, trauma, or limited access to resources. To create a more inclusive and equitable mental health landscape, it is imperative to prioritize the needs of the vulnerable.

Supporting the vulnerable entails:

1. **Equity and Inclusion:** Advocating for equitable access to mental healthcare and resources for all, regardless of their background or

circumstances.

2. **Trauma-Informed Care:** Promoting trauma-informed care that recognizes the impact of trauma on mental health and provides sensitive, supportive services.
3. **Cultural Competence:** Ensuring that mental health services are culturally competent and respectful of diverse backgrounds and beliefs.

Conclusion: A Call to Action

The time has come to stand together as a global community and champion mental health as a collective cause. We must break the silence, foster understanding, and empathy, improve access to care, and advocate for change. Together, we can create a world where mental health is a priority, where support is readily available, and where stigma and discrimination no longer hold sway.

This is a call to action, not just for today but for the future. It is a call for each of us to play our part, no matter how small, in the ongoing journey toward mental health equity and compassion. Let us be the change-makers, the advocates, and the voices that raise awareness, reduce stigma, and transform lives.

May we unite in the cause of mental health and forge a path to a brighter, more compassionate future.

Extra Helps

Solutions to address mental health challenges and promote mental well-being:

Breaking Stigma and Silence:

1. Promote open conversations about mental health.
2. Educate yourself and others about mental health.
3. Share personal stories to reduce stigma.
4. Support mental health awareness campaigns.
5. Encourage empathy and understanding.

Fostering Understanding:

1. Attend mental health workshops and seminars.
2. Read books and articles on mental health.
3. Engage in conversations with mental health professionals.
4. Foster empathy through active listening.
5. Challenge misconceptions and stereotypes.

Access to Care and Resources:

1. Advocate for improved mental healthcare funding.
2. Support policies for affordable mental health services.
3. Create mental health clinics in underserved areas.
4. Develop telehealth options for remote areas.
5. Establish crisis hotlines and online resources.

Support and Empathy:

1. Be a supportive listener for friends and loved ones.
2. Encourage seeking professional help when needed.
3. Offer practical assistance during challenging times.
4. Attend support groups or therapy sessions.
5. Share mental health resources and helplines.

Self-Care and Well-Being:

1. Prioritize self-care routines.
2. Maintain a balanced diet.
3. Engage in regular physical activity.
4. Get adequate sleep and rest.
5. Practice mindfulness and relaxation techniques.

Building Resilience:

1. Develop emotional regulation skills.
2. Cultivate a growth mindset.
3. Seek professional therapy or counseling.
4. Explore creative outlets like art or music.
5. Enhance problem-solving abilities.

Stress Management:

1. Identify stressors and triggers.
2. Practice stress-reduction techniques.
3. Create a stress-relief toolkit.
4. Set boundaries to manage stressors.
5. Use time management strategies.

Social Connection:

1. Cultivate meaningful relationships.
2. Attend social events and gatherings.
3. Volunteer in your community.
4. Join clubs or interest groups.
5. Build a support network.

Addiction Recovery:

1. Seek professional addiction treatment.
2. Attend support groups like AA or NA.
3. Develop healthy coping mechanisms.
4. Identify addiction triggers and avoid them.
5. Surround yourself with a sober support system.

Trauma Recovery:

1. Consider trauma-focused therapy.
2. Practice grounding techniques.
3. Engage in creative expression as therapy.
4. Build a support system for trauma survivors.
5. Foster a safe and nurturing environment.

These solutions encompass various aspects of mental health, from raising awareness and fostering understanding to promoting access to care, self-care, and recovery. Implementing these strategies can contribute to a more supportive and compassionate mental health landscape.

Conclusion

A Symphony of Hope for Mental Health

In the tapestry of our lives, mental health is the vibrant thread that weaves our experiences together. Let it be a thread of hope, compassion, and understanding.

As we reach the culmination of our exploration into the intricate world of mental health, we find ourselves standing on the precipice of transformation—a transformation not just of individuals but of societies, communities, and the world at large. We have journeyed through the depths of emotions, resilience, support, and action, all in pursuit of a brighter, more compassionate world for mental health.

Mental health is not a solitary endeavor; it is a symphony of experiences, emotions, and stories that resonate within us all. It is the symphony of hope that plays in the hearts of those who have faced adversity and emerged stronger. It is the symphony of compassion that extends a helping hand to those in need. It is the symphony of understanding that embraces the diversity of human experiences.

The Threads of Hope and Compassion

In this symphony, the threads of hope and compassion are interwoven with the fabric of human existence. Hope is the guiding star that lights our path, the belief that change is possible, and the resilience that carries us through turbulent times. Compassion is the gentle touch that soothes wounds, the understanding that fosters empathy, and the solidarity that reminds us that we are not alone on this journey.

Together, hope and compassion can unravel the knots of stigma, discrimination, and silence that have bound mental health for far too long. They can weave a new narrative—one that celebrates the strength of the human spirit, the power of vulnerability, and the beauty of diversity.

A Symphony of Understanding and Support

Understanding is the bridge that connects us, allowing us to see the world through the eyes of another. It is the realization that mental health is a universal language that transcends borders, cultures, and backgrounds. By fostering understanding, we pave the way for empathy—the cornerstone of support and compassion.

In this symphony, support is the harmony that lifts us when we falter. It is the network of friends, family, and professionals who stand with us during our darkest hours. Support is the embodiment of love, acceptance, and validation. It reminds us that seeking help is a sign of courage, not weakness, and that we are deserving of care and kindness.

The Ongoing Melody of Action

This symphony is not a static composition; it is an ongoing melody that requires action. It beckons us to break the silence surrounding mental health, to educate ourselves and others, and to advocate for change. It encourages us to create a world where access to care is equitable, stigma is shattered, and understanding is universal.

Action is the crescendo that empowers us to transform our communities and institutions. It is the force that propels us toward a future where mental health is prioritized, where individuals are supported in their journeys, and where every voice is heard. Action is the embodiment of resilience, determination, and the unwavering belief in the possibility of a better world.

A World of Resilience and Hope

In the grand symphony of life, mental health is not a mere note but a resounding chord that reverberates through every aspect of our existence. It is the chord of resilience, the melody of hope, and the harmony of compassion. As we conclude this symphony, may it serve as a reminder that mental health is a shared journey—one that we embark on together.

Let us continue to play our parts in this symphony of hope for mental health. Let us break the silence, foster understanding, support one another, and take action. Together, we can create a world where mental health is celebrated, where stigma is replaced with acceptance, and where every individual's well-being is valued.

As the symphony of mental health unfolds, may it be a testament to the strength of the human spirit, the power of community, and the enduring melody of hope. Let us listen to its tune and allow it to guide us toward a future where mental health is not just a thread but a vibrant tapestry of resilience, compassion, and understanding.

May this symphony resound in our hearts and inspire us to create a world where mental health thrives, and every individual finds the support and compassion they deserve.

Together, let us continue to compose this symphony, a symphony of hope for mental health.

ABOUT THE AUTHOR

Dr. José De La Rosa

- *Renowned Educator, Author, Advocate for Mental Health*

Introduction: Dr. José De La Rosa is more than just an accomplished educator, author, and polyglot—he is a compassionate advocate dedicated to making a difference in the lives of individuals grappling with mental health issues, particularly in challenging circumstances. Born in the Dominican Republic, Dr. De La Rosa has committed his career to not only educating and inspiring but also extending a helping hand to those facing depression and other mental health challenges.

Biography: Dr. José De La Rosa's journey is characterized by a profound dedication to the well-being of others. As a distinguished educator, he has nurtured minds, fostering a love for language and learning. His influence has extended beyond the classroom, impacting educational programs in over 30 countries, including Spanish-speaking regions in Latin America and Spain.

Literary Achievements: Dr. De La Rosa's literary repertoire encompasses a wide spectrum of subjects, reflecting his deep-seated commitment to education and culture. Among his celebrated works are "Wow Leadership," "Self-Esteem Encyclopedia," and the forthcoming "Mind Matters." These publications are not just about knowledge but also about providing solace and guidance to those navigating mental health challenges.

Global Recognition: His books have garnered international acclaim, recognized not only for their distinct writing style but also for the underlying message of hope and resilience—a message that resonates deeply with those facing mental health difficulties.

Multilingual Proficiency: Dr. De La Rosa's ability to communicate fluently in multiple languages, including Spanish, English, French, Italian, and Haitian Creole, serves as a bridge to connect with individuals from diverse backgrounds and cultures. This unique skill has played a vital role in promoting dialogue and cooperation, especially in the realm of mental health advocacy.

Passion for Mental Health: Embedded in every facet of Dr. De La Rosa's work is his unwavering passion for helping individuals, especially those submerged in the depths of mental health challenges and depression. He believes that education and understanding can shine a light on the path to healing and recovery.

Educational Philosophy: Through his written works and lectures, Dr. De La Rosa shares innovative ideas and methods for language instruction, advocating for the importance of bilingual and multicultural education. His approach focuses on making language learning not only enriching but also therapeutic a powerful tool for enhancing mental well-being.

Don't miss out!

Visit the website below and you can sign up to receive emails whenever Jose De La Rosa publishes a new book. There's no charge and no obligation.

https://books2read.com/r/B-A-NMSY-IOOVC

www.ingramcontent.com/pod-product-compliance
Lightning Source LLC
LaVergne TN
LVHW101617210926
848480LV00009B/773